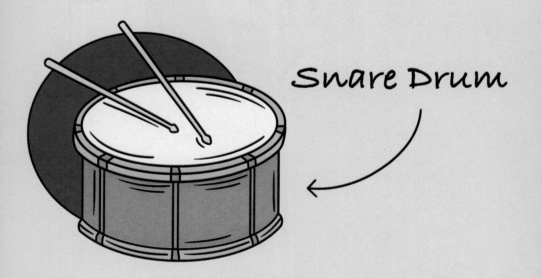

Snare Drum

This book belongs to:

_____

Dynamite

EXPLORE DRUMMING with

DYNAMITE DRUMS

and Bearific

KATELYN LONAS

Table of Contents

Introduction

Explore everything you need to know to become an outstanding drummer with Dynamite Drums.

Dynamite Drums is a company that is dedicated in teaching aspiring and beginner drummers.

History

Drums have existed for thousands of years and have evolved greatly through centuries of innovation.

One of the earliest evidences of drums can be traced back to 5500 B.C. During this time, Neolithic cultures

from China created drums
using alligator skin.

Ancient Mesopotamia and
Egypt invented frame
drums, which are drum
heads that are stretched over
a shallow wooden frame.

Around 600 B.C., the Dong Son civilization created the first bronze drum.

The bronze Dong Son drums are best known for their intricate designs, detailed engravings, and motifs.

These drums were used in musical performances, ceremonies, and symbolic offerings. Additionally, owning a bronze Dong Son drum was a sign of wealth and social status.

During the Middle Ages, kettledrums, also known as timpani, were widely popular and prominent in many regions of the world.

The modern drum set we know today emerged in the early twentieth century in New Orleans.

Music genres such as jazz, blues, and rock 'n' roll played pivotal roles in the evolution and refinement of the modern drum set.

In the early 1970s, the first electronic drum set was created by Graeme Edgein, who was the drummer of The Moody Blues.

This electronic drum set was used in the song Procession from the 1971 album Every Good Boy Deserves Favour.

However, electronic drums didn't become popular in both home recording and commercial studios until around the late 1980s.

Drum Set

A drum set is made up of several basic components.

This includes the bass drum, snare drum, tom-toms, hi-hat cymbals, crash cymbal, ride cymbal, and hardware such as pedals, stands, and a drum throne.

The bass drum is the largest piece of the drum set and is played using a foot pedal.

This part of the drum set is responsible for producing a very deep and low pitch that enhances the overall power of the music being played.

The snare drum sits on a special stand, and it has metal wires that vibrate when the drum is struck.

This part of the drum set produces a wide range of sounds, from sharp staccato hits to soft muffled sounds.

Tom-toms are cylindrical drums that can be single-headed or double-headed and come in a lot of sizes.

This part of the drum set is responsible for producing a rich sound, and it can be tuned to different pitches.

Hi-hat cymbals are two cymbals mounted on a stand, with one placed on top of the other.

This part of the drum set produces sharp sounds and varies between high pitches and deeper tones.

The crash cymbal is a single cymbal mounted on a stand and can come in many sizes.

This part of the drum set is responsible for producing loud, sharp, and explosive sounds that emphasize climactic moments in music.

The ride cymbal is a single cymbal mounted on a stand that is positioned on the right side of your drum set.

This part of the drum set produces a clear, bell-like tone and establishes a steady rhythm in music.

The hardware for a drum set includes stands that can be adjusted in height, as well as pedals to play the bass drum and hi-hat cymbals.

Additionally, all drum sets have a drum throne, which is a seat for the drummer.

Parts of a Drum Set

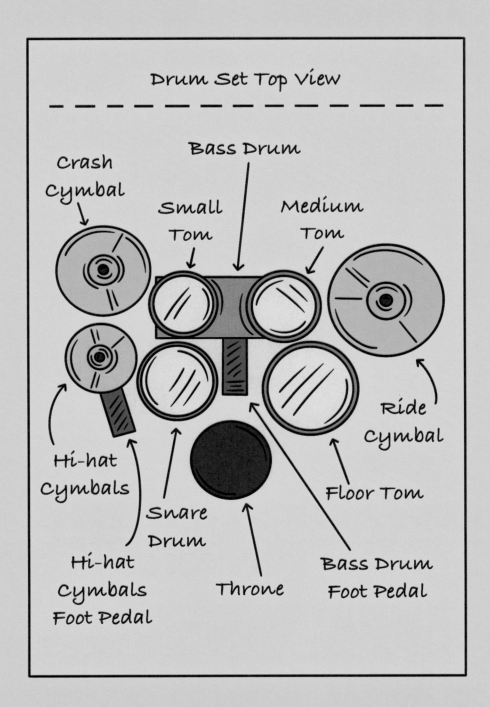

Drum Set Top View

Crash Cymbal

Bass Drum

Small Tom

Medium Tom

Ride Cymbal

Hi-hat Cymbals

Snare Drum

Floor Tom

Hi-hat Cymbals Foot Pedal

Throne

Bass Drum Foot Pedal

Drumsticks

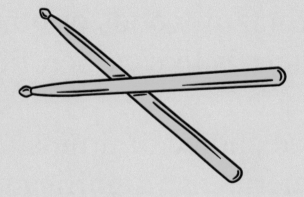

Many types of drumsticks are available for drummers.

However, standard drumsticks are the most common choice due to their versatility and adaptability across musical genres and playing techniques.

Standard drumsticks are usually made from a select group of woods or other materials like carbon fiber.

The choice of drumstick material can significantly impact the weight and sound produced while playing.

The most popular choices for drumsticks are made from hickory or maple.

There are six different kinds of drumheads, and they can change how the drumsticks feel when drumming.

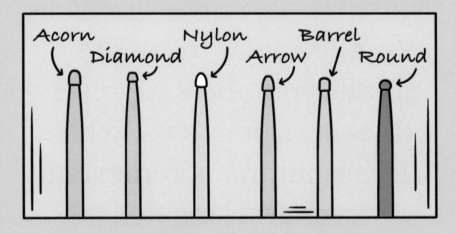

Drumheads are made from either wood or nylon.

Nylon tips sound bright, while wooden tips sound more natural.

Drumsticks are always marked with a combination of letters and numbers.

The numbers on drumsticks usually range from 1 to 9. Smaller numbers represent thicker drumsticks, while larger numbers represent thinner drumsticks.

The letter on drumsticks:
- S - is for symphonic use.
- A - is for orchestral use.
- B - is for band use.
- D - is for general use.

When using your drumsticks, be sure to put on your Dynamite Drumstick Grips!

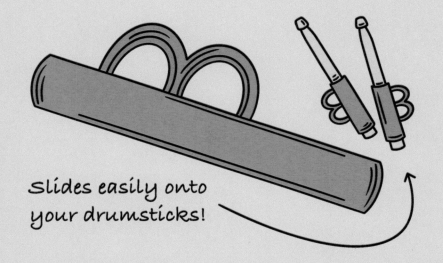

Slides easily onto your drumsticks!

The Dynamite Drumstick Grips helps you hold onto your drumsticks while playing the drums, and it was specially designed to assist beginner drummers.

Drum Notation

Drum notation is essential for drummers, as it provides a structured way to play drum beats and rhythms.

By mastering drum notation, you'll be able to write your own songs and accurately play your favorite songs.

Drum notation symbols are on a set of five horizontal lines called a staff.

Each part of the drum set is written on a line or between the spaces of lines.

The placement of drum notes corresponds to their pitch levels, with higher-pitched instruments like cymbals located at the top of the staff, while the bass drum and floor tom are on the bottom of the staff.

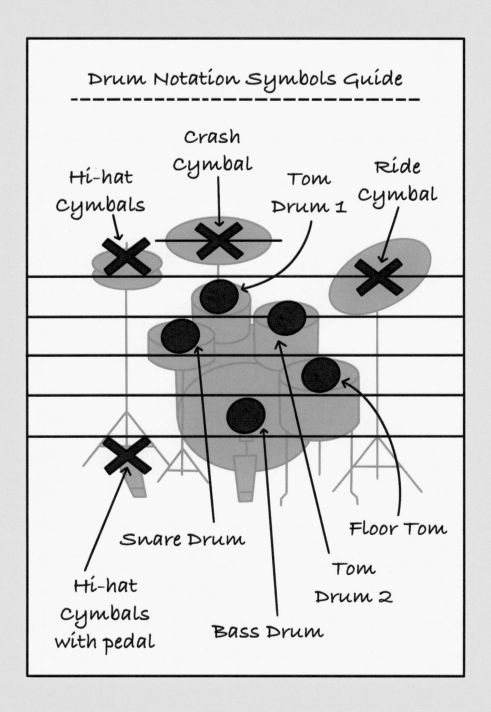

The time signatures and tempo can be found at the beginning on a staff before the drum notation symbols.

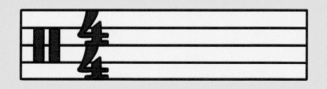

Time signatures indicate the number of beats in each measure and which note value receives one beat.

Tempos indicate how fast or slow the music should be played.

24

Types of tempo includes:
- Adagio: very slow tempo
- Andante: slow tempo
- Allegro: fast tempo
- Presto: very fast tempo

This is the basic knowledge you will need to understand about drum notation.

As you continue your drumming journey, you will come across other symbols, so consider using drum notation software to help you grasp new concepts.

Benefits

Playing the drums offers various benefits that can positively impact your life.

Drumming can improve your physical wellbeing as well as enhance your mental focus, cognitive skills, and creative skills.

Drumming improves bilateral coordination since it uses both hands and feet.

Regular practice of drumming can enhance hand-eye coordination and timing, as well as overall motor skill development.

Drumming is a physical activity that elevates your heart rate and improves your overall fitness level.

Additionally, playing the drums can help build muscle strength, specifically in the arms, shoulders, and core.

Drumming can act as a form of stress relief and promote a sense of mindfulness.

In addition, drumming can trigger the release of endorphins, which help alleviate stress and improve your overall mood.

Drumming encourages creativity and promotes problem solving, personal expression, and innovation.

It can also foster social connections and teamwork skills when joining a band or playing in a group.

Fun Facts

Drumming is one of the oldest musical activities.

By playing the drums, you can burn more calories in a half-hour session than you would in other physical exercises such as cycling, weightlifting, and hiking.

As of today, the largest drum in the world is called the Big Drum and is located in Germany. The Big Drum is over 40 feet tall and weighs around 20 tons.

The fastest drummer can reach a speed of 1,272 strokes in 60 seconds.

The sound certain types of drums produce can be heard from miles away, especially in open or outdoor environments.

The longest recorded drum session was accomplished in Canada, and it lasted 134 hours and 5 minutes.

The world's largest drum set includes 813 pieces and took approximately 36 years to complete.

The most expensive drum set in the world is Ringo Starr's Ludwig Oyster Black Pearl Drum Kit. This drum set was auctioned in 2015 for $2.2 million.

DD's Story

Dynamite Drums was founded by Skai Lonas, a talented drummer and entrepreneur who started his company at the age of 12.

Skai's passion for drumming began at a young age. When he was around 3 years old, his gōnggong (grandpa) in Taiwan saw his potential and encouraged him to pursue drumming.

This early support and guidance played a huge role in shaping Skai's journey towards becoming a successful drummer, and it was his determination and dedication to playing the drums that led him to the creation of his business, Dynamite Drums.

Skai's first drum set was a compact, 5-piece Roland HD-3 Electronic Drum Set.

One of Skai's first songs he played on the drums was called "Brown Sugar" by The Rolling Stones.

As Skai began to play the drums, he noticed how challenging it was to maintain a secure and proper grip on his drumsticks.

This observation inspired him to create a special drumstick grip designed to assist beginners in holding onto their drumsticks using a traditional grip.

This drumstick grip was made to improve grip control, technique, and comfort for drummers.

He believes that developing a secure and comfortable grip on the drumsticks allows drummers to play with more precision, power, and fluidity, contributing to their overall musical growth.

Today, Skai plays the drums on a 12-piece custom-made strawberry Gretsch drum set.

This strawberry Gretsch drum set holds historical significance as it was originally played by drummers from the bands Genesis, GTR, and Yes.

Skai's goal is to ignite a sense of enthusiasm and curiosity about drumming.

He hopes that by sharing his own personal experiences and insights, it will inspire readers to explore the world of drumming and appreciate the joy and creativity of all the amazing things playing the drums can bring.

Advice

It's crucial that you setup your drum set properly for optimal performance and be sure that all of your drums and cymbals are easily reachable.

While playing the drums, ensure you have the proper

drumming posture to
prevent any injuries.

Don't overtighten your
cymbals, because if they're
mounted too tight, they will
most likely crack.

When practicing drums, try
using a metronome, which
will help you keep a steady
rhythm and tempo.

Watch professional
drummers to learn new
techniques and enhance

your drumming skills.

Play the drums using your wrists, not your shoulders. When playing from your wrists, it allows you to conserve energy and have more leverage on the drumstick's rebound.

While learning new songs or drumming techniques, take your time and master the basics before trying to play fast. Remember, slow and steady beats fast and sloppy.

Pictures

Skai with his Strawberry
Gretsch Drum Set

Skai trying out the drums for
the first time

Skai drumming on his
Electronic Roland Drum Set

One of Skai's first drum sets

Skai's first prototype of his
Dynamite Drumstick Grip made
using tape and paper

Strawberry Gretsch Drum Set

Strawberry Gretsch Drum Set

Create

Create your own music and use the staff paper provided on the next few pages to notate your drum beats.

Use the drum notation symbols you learned on page 23 to assist you in creating your own music.

Create your own Music

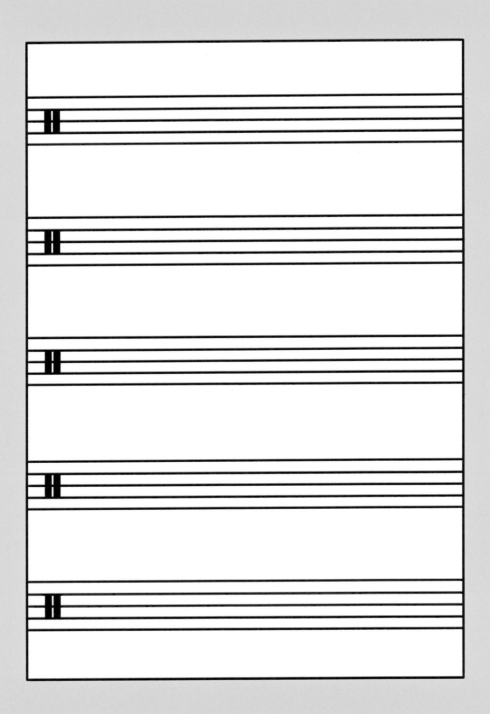

Create your own Music

Create your own Music

Create your own Music

Find more of Dynamite Drums on social media platforms like Instagram @dynamite.drums

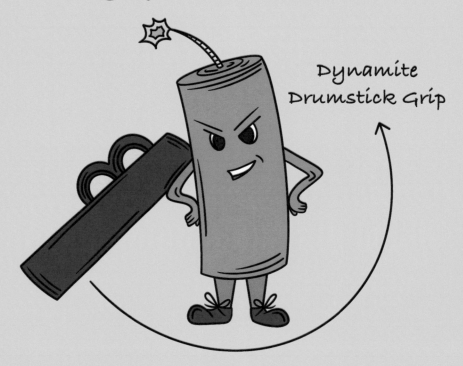

Dynamite Drumstick Grip

Get your own Dynamite Drumstick Grips at www.dynamitedrums.com

Dynamite Drums
- A book for Drummers -

The End!

remember to:

BELIEVE
DREAM
ACHIEVE

More Bearific books
on bearific.com

Author & Illustrator

Katelyn Lonas

Katelyn is 17 years old and resides in Southern California. Katelyn loves to encourage others to always believe in themselves and chase after their dreams! She began writing and illustrating her first book at age 9 and went on to publish 72 more books. She hopes you enjoyed this book and are excited for more to come!

— *Katelyn Lonas*

Made in the USA
Columbia, SC
02 June 2024

36296651R00044